PURGATORY

The publisher gratefully acknowledges the generous support
of the Joan Palevsky Literature in Translation Endowment Fund
of the University of California Press Foundation.

PURGATORY
RAÚL ZURITA

A BILINGUAL EDITION

TRANSLATED FROM THE SPANISH AND WITH AN AFTERWORD BY
ANNA DEENY
FOREWORD BY C.D. WRIGHT

UNIVERSITY OF CALIFORNIA PRESS   BERKELEY   LOS ANGELES   LONDON

University of California Press, one of the most distinguished university presses in the United States, enriches lives around the world by advancing scholarship in the humanities, social sciences, and natural sciences. Its activities are supported by the UC Press Foundation and by philanthropic contributions from individuals and institutions. For more information, visit www.ucpress.edu.

University of California Press
Berkeley and Los Angeles, California

University of California Press, Ltd.
London, England

Originally published as *Purgatorio*, by Editorial Universitaria, Chile, 1979.
First Universidad Diego Portales edition published in 2007.
Published in English and Spanish as *Purgatorio, 1970–1977* by the Latin American Literary Review Press, Pittsburgh, Pa., 1985.

LIBRARY OF CONGRESS CATALOGING-IN-PUBLICATION DATA

Zurita, Raúl.
  [Purgatorio, 1970–1977. English & Spanish]
  Purgatory / Raúl Zurita ; translated from the Spanish by Anna Deeny. — Bilingual ed.
    p.   cm.
  English and Spanish.
  Originally published in Spanish as *Purgatorio* in 1979.
  ISBN: 978-0-520-25972-0 (cloth : alk. paper)
  ISBN: 978-0-520-25973-7 (pbk. : alk. paper)
  1. Political persecution—Chile—Poetry.   2. Chile—Politics and government—1973–1988—Poetry.   I. Deeny, Anna, 1973–   II. Title.
PQ8098.36.U75P813   2009
861'.64—dc22   2009010981

Manufactured in the United States of America

18 17 16 15 14 13 12 11 10 09
10 9 8 7 6 5 4 3 2 1

This book is printed on Cascades Enviro 100, a 100% post consumer waste, recycled, de-inked fiber. FSC recycled certified and processed chlorine free. It is acid free, Ecologo certified, and manufactured by BioGas energy.

CONTENTS

Foreword by C. D. Wright   VII

Preface: Some Words for This Edition   XI

PURGATORY   1

Notes   97

Translator's Afterword: Speaking from the Wreckage   101

FOREWORD

Purgatory is, in all likelihood, the seminal literary text of Chile's 9/11/1973, the date of the U.S.-backed military coup led by Augusto Pinochet that overthrew the democratically elected government of Salvador Allende. With this first published collection of poems, the young Chilean poet Raúl Zurita began his Dantesque trilogy, his long, arduous pilgrimage toward earthly redemption. "Even if the evidence at hand might indicate that such a pursuit is folly," Zurita would later write, "we should keep on proposing Paradise."

His *obra* began in conflict, the poet tormented by his own image, his self-loathing countered by an aspiration toward divine love. Setting his words at odds with one another—angels versus bitches, humble supplication versus invective, ongoingness versus desperation—he wrote a profanely transcendent book. Despite the savage despair he experienced while writing *Purgatory,* Zurita matched despair with ferocity, deploying his own formal inventiveness and skill to compose the poem that would stand as both a subwoofer attack on tyranny and a work of never-ending strangeness. Since its debut six years into the Pinochet dictatorship, the Spanish-language edition of this fiery, uncategorizable book has never gone out of print.

In a national crisis, not everyone goes into exile; indeed not everyone has the option. Nor does everyone else disappear or die or meld with the silent majority. Neither is anyone spared. Thus, along with cadres of others opposed to Pinochet, Raúl Zurita—the young husband and father, the former engineering student—was assigned his defining, historical moment. Perforce, Zurita created his groundbreaking document in a quake-and-coup-marked country: Chile, the sky over Chile, the desert, the marked, mewling cows, Citizen Rachel, and even his own Chilean body, became his manuscript. Following the publication of the second book of Zurita's trilogy, *Anteparaíso* (1982), Steven F. White would declare, "New Chilean poetry is being measured in terms of Raúl Zurita" (*Poets of Chile*).

Purgatory suggests a topo map of the majestic country, while the poet bears the scar that runs through it. Instead of speaking for others, Zurita channels their voices. The poem opens with a speaker admitting that her friends think she is sick because she has disfigured her own face. A photo of Zurita's own self-injured face follows, the headshot of an identification card, and below it, the text "EGO SUM." On the next page, written by hand, a woman addresses the reader, perhaps the same speaker as the first or perhaps another of the starkly differing voices in the poem: "Me llamo Raquel" (My name is Rachel). In full capital letters, below the handwritten text, the last line on the page reads "QUI SUM."

From the first pages the poem crosses a frontier, entering a geography where things are not what they seem, where people are not who they claim, and where ordinary citizens have lost their way. The destination is not Paradise but the beach of Purgatory, Chile's Atacama, a part of which climatologists have designated absolute desert. Atacama, driest place on earth, site of the ultimate challenge—the creation of a tenable language, one that does not succumb to the official lies. Atacama, the brilliant, immaculate, blinding blank page. Atacama, from which the broken column, the fleeing herd, the abandoned Christ, Zurita and his friends can at least cry out, *eli eli* . . . the landscape as acute as the extremities of Zurita's expression.

Midway along the unguided path of Purgatory, a handwritten letter from a psychologist is inserted into the poem, a diagnosis of epileptic psychosis. The patient's name, Raúl Zurita, has been scratched out, the names Violeta, Dulce Beatriz, Rosamund, Manuela written above and below.

In the final pages, "three anonymous encephalograms" record the persistent sputterings of a mind under duress.

From the beginning to the end of the Pinochet regime, Zurita's actions, private and public, have ranged from the horrible to the sublime. He has performed terrible acts of self-mutilation, branding his face and burning his eyes with ammonia, but he has also inscribed the sky and the desert with his poetry. On June 2, 1982, his poem "La vida nueva," which opens *Anteparaíso,* appeared in Spanish above New York City, an act that, at that time, would have been impossible in Chile:

MI DIOS ES HAMBRE	*MY GOD IS HUNGER*
MI DIOS ES NIEVE	*MY GOD IS SNOW*
MI DIOS ES NO	*MY GOD IS NO*
MI DIOS ES DESENGAÑO	*MY GOD IS DISILLUSIONMENT*
MI DIOS ES CARROÑA . . .	*MY GOD IS CARRION . . .*

And in the Atacama Desert the last four words of the third volume in Zurita's trilogy, *La vida nueva,* have been bulldozed into the earth, stretching almost two miles:

ni pena ni miedo	*neither pain nor fear*

Zurita's internal exile whet his resistance, censorship kindling within him radical forms of creativity. Under the eyes of church and dictatorship, he began to write and publish his poetry, juxtaposing secular and sacred, ruled and unruled. With a mysterious admixture of logic and logos, Christian symbols, brain scans, graphics, and a medical report, Zurita expanded the formal repertoire of his language, of poetic materials, pushing back against the ugly vapidity of rule by force. A subversively original book, *Purgatory* is as coded as Gertrude Stein's *Lifting Belly,* delirious as Allen Ginsberg's *Howl,* and textured as Theresa Hak Kyung Cha's *Dictée.*

Time has not tempered the poet's ideals, and poetry has not forsaken him. Zurita's writings, his *obra,* continue to build their strata of significance. Raúl Zurita has remained mindfully undistracted from his original task of transcending the unbearable through art and of proposing the possibility of Paradise even in the face of unimaginable suffering.

At the outset of his journey through *Purgatory,* Zurita writes, "Life is very beautiful, even now." It is. Isn't it. Isn't it.

C. D. Wright

PREFACE: SOME WORDS FOR THIS EDITION

As if poems were the earth's dreams. Sometimes it appears that poems are this: the earth's dreams. I lived seventeen years under Pinochet's dictatorship, and imagining these poems occupying landscapes was my intimate form of resistance, of not giving up, of not dying in the midst of abuse and confinement. When faced with the horror, we had to respond with art that was stronger and more vast than the pain and damage inflicted on us. I believe this is what I thought in 1975, a year and a half after the military coup. It was then that a few soldiers subjected me to one of those typical abuses in which they are experts. I recalled the well-known evangelical phrase: if someone strikes your right cheek, turn the other to him. So I burned my left cheek. Completely alone, I enclosed myself in a bathroom and burned it with a red-hot branding iron.

Purgatory began with that laceration. It was my first book and was published four years later, in 1979. Almost at the same time, I envisioned poems drawing themselves in the sky. Three years later, when a few of those poems were written over New York City (the photographs are in my second book, *Anteparadise*), I thought that what had begun in utmost solitude and anguish had to conclude one day with the prospect of happiness. It's difficult for me to comment on my own work, but I feel that *Purgatory* represents a certain image of what pain can generate, of its desperation, but also, I hope, of its beauty.

It seemed to me then that the great imprints of human passion, of our suffering, as well as a strange perpetuity and survival, are reflected in the landscape. None of the poetic forms I knew, nothing, could help me express this. From there, I think, emerged the need to use other registers, such as mathematics (I was finishing my studies in engineering when the

XI

coup d'état occurred in Chile, studies I was unable to complete because of my arrest) or visual forms or documents. It has also occurred to me that everything I've done either well or inadequately since is an extension of *Purgatory* zones, as if the book were written to represent a memory.

I had to learn to speak again from total wreckage, almost from madness, so that I could still say something to someone. I think that *Purgatory* is evidence of that wreckage and of that learning. Writing this book was my private form of resurrection. An example of this process can be found in a psychiatric report to which I added "I love you I love you infinitely." Yes, this is what it means: to be able to say something to someone else, even from the most profound place of humiliation and shame. Almost thirty years later, I imagined a poem written over the great cliffs facing the Pacific and felt surprised to be alive, surprised that so much time had passed and that I could see the ocean.

Purgatory is not much more than this. In a more benign world, art would no longer be necessary, because each particle of life, every human emotion, would be in itself a poem, the vastest of symphonies, a mural of skies, the cordilleras, the Pacific, the seashores and deserts. Then, between poetry and love, we would not require the mediation of words.

Raúl Zurita
Santiago, 2009

PURGATORY

mis amigos creen que
estoy   muy   mala
porque quemé mi mejilla

my   friends   think
I'm   a   sick   woman
because I burned my cheek

DEVOCIÓN

A Diamela Eltit: la
santísima trinidad y la
pornografía

"LA VIDA ES MUY HERMOSA, INCLUSO AHORA"

DEVOTION

To Diamela Eltit: the
most holy trinity and
pornography

"LIFE IS VERY BEAUTIFUL, EVEN NOW"

EN EL MEDIO DEL CAMINO

IN THE MIDDLE OF THE ROAD

EGO SUM

Me llamo Raquel
estoy en el oficio
desde hace varios
años. Me encuentro
en la mitad de
mi vida. Perdí
el camino.—

QUI SUM

My name is Rachel
I've been in the same
business for many
years. I'm in the
middle of my life.
I lost my way.—

DOMINGO EN LA MAÑANA

I

Me amanezco
Se ha roto una columna

Soy una santa   digo

SUNDAY MORNING

I

I awake
A column has broken

I am a sainted woman   I say

III

Todo maquillado contra los vidrios
me llamé esta iluminada dime que no
el Súper Estrella de Chile
me toqué en la penumbra   besé mis piernas

Me he aborrecido tanto estos años

XIII

Yo soy el confeso   mírame   la Inmaculada
Yo he tiznado de negro
a las monjas y los curas

Pero ellos me levantan sus sotanas
Debajo sus ropas siguen blancas

—Ven, somos las antiguas novias   me dicen

III

All made-up face against the glass
I called myself this enlightened woman tell me it's not so
the Super Star of Chile
I touched myself in the shadows   I kissed my legs

I've hated myself so much these years

XIII

I am the convert   look at me   the Immaculata
I've sullied the nuns
and priests

But they lift their cassocks to show me
Beneath their clothes remain white

—Come, we're the ancient brides   they say

XXII

Destrocé mi cara tremenda
frente al espejo

te amo —me dije— te amo
Te amo a más que nada en el mundo

XXXIII

Les aseguro que no estoy enfermo   créanme
ni me suceden a menudo estas cosas
pero pasó que estaba en un baño
cuando vi algo como un ángel
"Cómo estás, perro" le oí decirme
Bueno —eso sería todo
Pero ahora los malditos recuerdos
ya no me dejan ni dormir por las noches

XXII

I smashed my sickening face
in the mirror
I love you —I said— I love you

I love you more than anything in the world

XXXIII

I'm telling you I'm not sick   believe me
these things don't even happen to me
very often but this one time in a bathroom
I saw something like an angel
"How are you, dog" I heard him say
Well —that's all
But now the goddamned memories
keep me up at night

XXXVIII

Sobre los riscos de la ladera: el sol
entonces abajo en el valle
la tierra cubierta de flores
Zurita enamorado amigo
recoge el sol de la fotosíntesis
Zurita ya no será nunca más amigo
desde la 7 P.M. ha empezado a anochecer

La noche es el manicomio de las plantas

XLII

Encerrado entre las cuatro paredes de
un baño: miré hacia el techo
entonces empecé a lavar las paredes y
el piso el lavatorio   el mismo baño
Es que vean: Afuera el cielo era Dios
y me chupaba el alma —sí hombre!
Me limpiaba los empañados ojos

XXXVIII

Over the cliffs of the hillside: the sun
then below in the valley
the earth covered with flowers
Zurita enamored friend
takes in the sun of photosynthesis
Zurita will now never again be friend
since 7 P.M. it's been getting dark

Night is the insane asylum of the plants

XLII

Enclosed within the four walls of
a bathroom: I looked up at the ceiling
and began to clean the walls and
the floor the sink   all of it
You see: Outside the sky was God
and he was sucking at my soul —believe me!
I wiped my weeping eyes

LVII

En la angosta cama desvencijada
desvelado toda la noche
como una vela apagada vuelta a encender
creí ver a Buddha varias veces
Sentí a mi lado el jadeo de una mujer
pero Buddha eran los almohadones
y la mujer está durmiendo el sueño eterno

LXIII

Hoy soñé que era Rey
me ponían una piel a manchas blancas y negras
Hoy mujo con mi cabeza a punto de caer
mientras las campanadas fúnebres de la iglesia
dicen que va a la venta la leche

LVII

In the narrow broken bed
restless all night
like a spent candle lit again
I thought I saw Buddha many times
At my side I felt a woman's gasp for air
but Buddha was only the pillows
and the woman is sleeping the eternal dream

LXIII

Today I dreamed that I was King
they were dressing me in black-and-white spotted pelts
Today I moo with my head about to fall
as the church bells' mournful clanging
says that milk goes to market

LXXXV

Me han rapado la cabeza
me han puesto estos harapos de lana gris
—mamá sigue fumando
Yo soy Juana de Arco

Me registran con microfilms

XCII

El vidrio es transparente como el agua
Pavor de los prismas y los vidrios
Yo doy vuelta la luz para no perderme en ellos

LXXXV

They've shaved my head
they've dressed me in these gray wool rags
—Mom keeps on smoking
I am Joan of Arc

They catalog me on microfilm

XCII

The glass is transparent like water
Dread of prisms and glass
I circle the light so as not to lose myself in them

DOMINGO EN LA MAÑANA / EPÍLOGO

⊏

Se ha roto una columna: vi a Dios
aunque no lo creas te digo
sí hombre   ayer domingo
con los mismos ojos de este vuelo

SUNDAY MORNING / EPILOGUE

C

A column has broken: I saw God
even if you don't believe it I'm telling you
it's true   yesterday Sunday
with the same eyes of this flight

DESIERTOS

DESERTS

COMO UN SUEÑO

Claro: este es el Desierto
de Atacama   buena cosa   no
valía ni tres chauchas llegar
allí y no has visto el
Desierto de Atacama —oye:
lo viste allá cierto? bueno
si no lo has visto anda de
una vez y no me jodas

LAPSUS Y ENGAÑOS SE LLAMAN MI PROPIA MENTE EL
DESIERTO DE CHILE

LIKE A DREAM

Of course: this is the Desert
of Atacama   impressive   it didn't
cost a dime to get there
and you haven't seen the
Desert of Atacama —listen:
you saw it out there didn't you?
well if you haven't seen it
just go once and for all and
leave me the fuck alone

LAPSES AND DECEITS ARE CALLED MY OWN MIND THE
DESERT OF CHILE

COMO UN SUEÑO

Mirá qué cosa: el Desierto de
Atacama son puras manchas
sabías?   claro   pero no te
costaba nada mirarte un poco
también a ti mismo y decir:
Anda yo también soy una buena
mancha Cristo —oye lindo   no
has visto tus pecados?   bien
pero entonces déjalo mejor
encumbrarse por esos cielos
manchado   como en tus sueños

COMO ESPEJISMOS Y AURAS EL INRI ES MI MENTE EL
DESIERTO DE CHILE

LIKE A DREAM

Look at that: the Desert of
Atacama it's nothing but stains
did you know?   of course   but how
hard would it have been to
take a look at yourself and say:
Christ come on I too am full of
stains —listen pretty boy   have you
seen your own sins?   good
but then allow him to better lift
himself through those skies
stained   like in your dreams

LIKE MIRAGES AND AURAS THE INRI IS MY MIND THE
DESERT OF CHILE

COMO UN SUEÑO

Vamos: no quisiste saber nada de
ese Desierto maldito —te dio
miedo   yo sé que te dio miedo
cuando supiste que se había
internado por esas cochinas
pampas —claro no quisiste
saber nada pero se te volaron
los colores de la cara y bueno
dime: te creías que era poca
cosa enfilarse por allá para
volver después de su propio
nunca   dado vuelta   extendido
como una llanura frente a nosotros

YO USTED Y LA NUNCA SOY LA VERDE PAMPA EL
DESIERTO DE CHILE

LIKE A DREAM

Come on: you didn't want to know
anything about that damned Desert —it
scared you   I know it scared you
when you found out it'd been
overrun by those filthy
pampas —of course you didn't want
to know anything but the colors
vanished from your face and OK
say it: did you think it was
no big deal to go all the way there
just to return then from your own
never   turned around   extended
like a plain before us

I YOU AND NEVER I AM THE GREEN PAMPA THE
DESERT OF CHILE

EL DESIERTO DE ATACAMA

THE DESERT OF ATACAMA

QUIEN PODRÍA LA ENORME DIGNIDAD DEL
DESIERTO DE ATACAMA COMO UN PÁJARO
SE ELEVA SOBRE LOS CIELOS APENAS
EMPUJADO POR EL VIENTO

WHO COULD THE ENORMOUS DIGNITY OF
THE DESERT OF ATACAMA LIKE A BIRD
IT ELEVATES ITSELF OVER THE SKIES BARELY
PRESSED BY THE WIND

I

A LAS INMACULADAS LLANURAS

i. Dejemos pasar el infinito del Desierto de Atacama

ii. Dejemos pasar la esterilidad de estos desiertos

Para que desde las piernas abiertas de mi madre se
levante una Plegaria que se cruce con el infinito del
Desierto de Atacama y mi madre no sea entonces sino
un punto de encuentro en el camino

iii. Yo mismo seré entonces una Plegaria encontrada
en el camino

iv. Yo mismo seré las piernas abiertas de mi madre

Para cuando vean alzarse ante sus ojos los desolados
paisajes del Desierto de Atacama mi madre se concentre
en gotas de agua y sea la primera lluvia en el desierto

v. Entonces veremos aparecer el Infinito del Desierto

vi. Dado vuelta desde sí mismo hasta dar con las piernas
de mi madre

vii. Entonces sobre el vacío del mundo se abrirá
completamente el verdor infinito del Desierto de
Atacama

I

TO THE IMMACULATE PLAINS

i.   Let's let the infinity of the Desert of Atacama pass

ii. Let's let the sterility of these deserts pass

So that from the spread-open legs of my mother a Prayer
rises that intersects the infinity of the Desert of Atacama
and my mother is then nothing but a meeting point on the road

iii. Then I myself will be a Prayer found on the road

iv. I myself will be the spread-open legs of my mother

So that when they see raised up before their eyes the desolate
landscapes of the Desert of Atacama my mother will be
concentrated in drops of water as the first rain of the desert

v.   Then we'll see the Infinity of the Desert appear

vi. Turned around itself until striking my mother's legs

vii. Then over the world's emptiness the infinite green of the
     Desert of Atacama will open completely

EL DESIERTO DE ATACAMA II

Helo allí   Helo allí
suspendido en el aire
El Desierto de Atacama

i.   Suspendido   sobre el cielo de Chile   diluyéndose
     entre auras

ii. Convirtiendo esta vida y la otra en el mismo
     Desierto de Atacama   áurico   perdiéndose en el
     aire

iii. Hasta que finalmente no haya cielo sino Desierto
     de Atacama y todos veamos entonces nuestras
     propias pampas fosforescentes carajas
     encumbrándose en el horizonte

THE DESERT OF ATACAMA II

There   it   is   There
suspended   in   the air
The Desert of Atacama

i.   Suspended   over the sky of Chile   dissolving
     amid auras

ii. Converting this life and the other into the same
     Desert of Atacama   luminous   losing itself in the
     air

iii. Until finally there's not sky but only Desert of
     Atacama and then all of us will see our own fucked
     phosphorescent pampas soaring in the horizon

EL DESIERTO DE ATACAMA III

i. Los desiertos de atacama son azules

ii. Los desiertos de atacama no son azules   ya ya dime
    lo que quieras

iii. Los desiertos de atacama no son azules porque por
     allá no voló el espíritu de J. Cristo que era un perdido

iv. Y si los desiertos de atacama fueran azules todavía
    podrían ser el Oasis Chileno para que desde todos
    los rincones de Chile contentos viesen flamear por
    el aire las azules pampas del Desierto de Atacama

THE DESERT OF ATACAMA III

i. The deserts of atacama are blue

ii. The deserts of atacama aren't blue   go ahead say
what you will

iii. The deserts of atacama aren't blue because
out there J. Christ's spirit didn't fly he was lost

iv. And if the deserts of atacama were blue still
they could be the Chilean Oasis so that from every
corner of Chile gladly you'd see flaming through
the air the blue pampas of the Desert of Atacama

EL DESIERTO DE ATACAMA IV

i.   El Desierto de Atacama son puros pastizales

ii. Miren a esas ovejas correr sobre los pastizales del
     desierto

iii. Miren a sus mismos sueños balar allá sobre esas
     pampas infinitas

iv. Y si no se escucha a las ovejas balar en el Desierto
     de Atacama nosotros somos entonces los pastizales
     de Chile para que en todo el espacio en todo el mundo
     en toda la patria se escuche ahora el balar de nuestras
     propias almas sobre esos desolados desiertos miserables

THE DESERT OF ATACAMA IV

i. The Desert of Atacama is nothing but pastures

ii. Look at those sheep run across the desert pastures

iii. Look at their very dreams bleat over there throughout those
    infinite pampas

iv. And if you don't listen to the sheep bleat in the
    Desert of Atacama then do we become the pastures
    of Chile so that everywhere   all over the world
    all over the country you listen now to our own souls
    bleat throughout those miserable desolate deserts

EL DESIERTO DE ATACAMA V

Di tú del silbar de Atacama
el viento borra como nieve
el color de esa llanura

i. El Desierto de Atacama sobrevoló infinidades de
    desiertos para estar allí

ii. Como el viento siéntanlo silbando pasar entre el
    follaje de los árboles

iii. Mírenlo transparentarse allá lejos   y sólo
     acompañado por el viento

iv. Pero cuidado: porque si al final el Desierto de
    Atacama no estuviese donde debiera estar el
    mundo entero comenzaría a silbar entre el follaje
    de los árboles   y nosotros nos veríamos entonces
    en el mismísimo nunca   transparentes   silbantes
    en el viento tragándonos el color de esta pampa

THE DESERT OF ATACAMA V

Speak of the whistle of Atacama
the wind erases like snow
the color of that plain

i.   The Desert of Atacama soared over infinities of
     deserts to be there

ii. Like the wind feel it pass whistling through the
     leaves of the trees

iii. Look at it become transparent faraway   and just
     accompanied by the wind

iv. But be careful: because if ultimately the Desert
     of Atacama were not where it should be the
     whole world would begin to whistle through the
     leaves of the trees   and then we'd see ourselves
     in the same never   transparent   whistles
     in the wind swallowing the color of this pampa

EL DESIERTO DE ATACAMA VI

No sueñen las áridas llanuras
Nadie ha podido ver nunca
Esas pampas quiméricas

i. Los paisajes son convergentes y divergentes en el
Desierto de Atacama

ii. Sobre los paisajes convergentes y divergentes Chile
es convergente y divergente en el Desierto de Atacama

iii. Por eso lo que está allá nunca estuvo allá y si ese
siguiese donde está vería darse vuelta su propia
vida hasta ser las quiméricas llanuras   desérticas
iluminadas   esfumándose como ellos

iv. Y cuando vengan a desplegarse los paisajes
convergentes y divergentes del Desierto de
Atacama Chile entero habrá sido el más allá de la
vida   porque a cambio de Atacama ya se están
extendiendo como un sueño los desiertos de
nuestra propia quimera allá en estos llanos del
demonio

THE DESERT OF ATACAMA VI

Arid plains do not dream
No one has ever managed to see
Those chimerical pampas

i. The landscapes are convergent and divergent in the
   Desert of Atacama

ii. Over the convergent and divergent landscapes Chile
    is convergent and divergent in the Desert of Atacama

iii. That's why what's there never was there and if it
     were to stay where it is it would see its own life turn
     around until being the chimerical plains   deserted
     enlightened   fading away like them

iv. And when the convergent and divergent landscapes
    of the Desert of Atacama unfold themselves
    all of Chile will have been the life beyond   because
    unlike Atacama they are already extending themselves
    like a dream the deserts of our own chimera
    over there in these plains of hell

EL DESIERTO DE ATACAMA VII

i.   Miremos entonces el Desierto de Atacama

ii. Miremos nuestra soledad en el desierto

Para que desolado frente a estas fachas el paisaje
devenga una cruz extendida sobre Chile y la soledad de mi
facha vea entonces el redimirse de las otras fachas: mi
propia Redención en el Desierto

iii. Quién diría entonces del redimirse de mi facha

iv. Quién hablaría de la soledad del desierto

Para que mi facha comience a tocar tu facha y tu facha
a esa otra facha y así hasta que todo Chile no sea sino
una sola facha con los brazos abiertos: una larga facha
coronada de espinas

v.   Entonces la Cruz no será sino el abrirse de brazos
     de mi facha

vi. Nosotros seremos entonces la Corona de Espinas
     del Desierto

vii. Entonces   clavados facha con facha   como una Cruz
     extendida sobre Chile   habremos visto para siempre
     el Solitario Expirar del Desierto de Atacama

THE DESERT OF ATACAMA VII

i.   Let's look then at the Desert of Atacama

ii. Let's look at our loneliness in the desert

So that desolate before these forms the landscape becomes
a cross extended over Chile and the loneliness of my form
then sees the redemption of the other forms: my own
Redemption in the Desert

iii. Then who would speak of the redemption of my form

iv. Who would tell of the desert's loneliness

So that my form begins to touch your form and your form
that other form like that until all of Chile is nothing but
one form with open arms: a long form crowned with thorns

v.   Then the Cross will be nothing but the opening arms
     of my form

vi. We will then be the Crown of Thorns in the Desert

vii. Then   nailed form to form   like a Cross
     extended over Chile   we will have seen forever
     the Final Solitary Breath of the Desert of Atacama

EPÍLOGO

COMO UN SUEÑO EL SILBADO DEL VIENTO
TODAVÍA RECORRE EL ÁRIDO ESPACIO DE
ESAS LLANURAS

EPILOGUE

LIKE A DREAM THE WHISTLE OF THE
WIND STILL TRAVERSES THE ARID
SPACE OF THOSE PLAINS

ARCOSANTO

HOLY ARCH

LA GRUTA DE
LOURDES

Otto:

Te ~~permitir~~ una impresión sobre (la)
~~el~~ paciente ~~Luisa Irena~~ dado el mal es-
tado en que *Dulce Beatriz* se encuentra. Los resulta-
dos especial- *Rosamunda* Rorschach coinciden
mente *Manuela*
plenamente con tu diagnóstico observán-
dose numerosos elementos positivos de
psicósis de tipo epiléptico. El caso
es muy interezante y me gustaría
saber si hay o no corroboración con
el EEG y si existe foco.-

El informe detallado lo tendré
el Lunes próximo.

atte,

4/5/74.-

Ana María Alessandra
Psychologist

THE GROTTO OF LOURDES

Otto:

I'm forwarding my impression regarding the patient ~~Raúl Zurita~~/ Violeta /
Sweet Beatriz / Rosamunda / Manuela given the state in which ~~he's~~ (she's)
in. The results, especially the Rorschach, coincide entirely with your
diagnosis revealing many elements that indicate an epileptic psychosis.
The case is very interesting and I'd like to know if the EEG corroborates
or not these findings and if a focus exists.

I'll have the detailed report next Monday.

Sincerely,
Ana María Alessandri

5/4/74

OVE YOU I LOVE YOU INFINITELY I L

ÁREAS VERDES

GREEN AREAS

NO EL INMENSO YACER DE LA VACA
bajo las estrellas su cabeza pasta sobre el
campo su cola silba en el aire   sus mugidos
no   alcanzan a cubrir las pampas de su silencio

NOT THE IMMENSE REPOSE OF THE COW
below the stars her head grazes throughout
the field   her tail   hums in the air   her   moos
cannot   comprehend the pampas of her silence

Han visto extenderse estos pastos infinitos?

I. Han visto extenderse esos pastos infinitos
    donde las vacas huyendo desaparecen
    reunidas   ingrávidas   delante de ellos?

II. No hay domingos para la vaca:
    mugiendo despierta en un espacio vacío
    babeante   gorda   sobre esos pastos imaginarios

Have you seen these infinite pastures extend themselves?

I. Have you seen those infinite pastures extend themselves
    where the cows fleeing disappear
    reunited   weightless   before them?

II. There are no Sundays for the cow:
    mooing awake in a hollow space
    drooling   heavy   throughout those imaginary pastures

Comprended las fúnebres manchas de la vaca
los vaqueros
lloran frente a esos nichos

I.   Esta vaca es una insoluble paradoja
     pernocta bajo las estrellas
     pero se alimenta de logos
     y sus manchas finitas son símbolos

II. Esa otra   en cambio   odia los colores:
     se fué a pastar a un tiempo
     donde el único color que existe es el negro

Ahora los vaqueros no saben qué hacer con esa
vaca pues sus manchas no son otra cosa
que la misma sombra de sus perseguidores

Do you understand the funereal spots of the cow
the cowboys
weep before those recesses

I. This cow is an insoluble paradox
    she spends the night under the stars
    but nourishes herself with logos
    and her finite spots are symbols

II. That other one   however   hates colors:
     once she went to graze
     where the only color that exists is black

Now the cowboys don't know what to do with
that cow because her spots are nothing
but the shadow itself of her persecutors

Las había visto pastando en el radiante   λόγος?

I. Algunas vacas se perdieron en la lógica

II. Otras huyeron por un subespacio
    donde solamente existen biologías

III. Esas otras   finalmente   vienen vagando
     desde hace como un millón de años
     pero no podrán ser nunca vistas por sus vaqueros
     pues viven en las geometrías no euclideanas

Had you seen them grazing in the radiant λόγος?

I. Some cows were lost in the logic

II. Others fled through a subspace
where only biologies exist

III. Those others   finally   come wandering
as if from a million years ago
but they'll never be able to be seen by their cowboys
because they live in the non-Euclidean geometries

Vamos el increíble acoso de la vaca
La muerte
no turba su mirada

I. Sus manchas finalmente
van a perderse en otros mundos

II. Esa vaca muge pero morirá y su mugido será
"Eli Eli / lamma sabacthani" para que el
vaquero le dé un lanzazo en el costado y esa
lanza llegue al más allá

III. Sabía Ud. que las manchas de esas vacas
quedarán vacías y que los vaqueros estarán
entonces en el otro mundo videntes laceando en
esos hoyos malditos?

Come on the incredible hunt for the cow
Death
does not trouble her gaze

I. Her spots will finally
   lose their way in other worlds

II. That cow moos but she'll die and her mooing will be
    "Eli Eli / lamma sabacthani"   so that the
    cowboy will spear her side and that
    spearing will reach the beyond

III. Did you know that the spots of those cows will
     hollow and the cowboys will then be in the other
     world   prophets   lassoing within those damned holes?

Sabía Ud. algo de las verdes áreas regidas?

Sabía Ud. algo de las verdes áreas regidas por los
vaqueros y las blancas áreas no regidas que las vacas
huyendo dejan compactas   cerradas   detrás de ellas?

I.   Esa área verde regida se intersecta con la
     primera área blanca no regida

II. Ese cruce de áreas verdes y blancas se intersecta
     con la segunda área blanca no regida

III. Las áreas verdes regidas y las blancas áreas no
     regidas se siguen intersectando hasta acabarse las
     áreas blancas no regidas

Sabía Ud. que ya sin áreas que se intersecten comienzan
a cruzarse todos los símbolos entre sí y que es Ud.
ahora el área blanca que las vacas huyendo dejan a
merced del área del más allá de Ud.   verde   regida por los
mismos vaqueros locos?

Did you know anything about the patrolled green areas?

Did you know anything about the green areas patrolled by
the cowboys and the unpatrolled white areas that
the cows fleeing leave compact   closed   behind them?

I.   That patrolled green area intersects with the
     first unpatrolled white area

II. That crisscross of green and white areas intersects
     with the second unpatrolled white area

III. The patrolled green areas and the unpatrolled
     white areas continue intersecting until the
     unpatrolled white areas end

Did you know that now without areas that intersect each
other all of the symbols begin to crisscross themselves
among themselves and that you are now the white area that
the cows fleeing leave at the mercy of the area of the
beyond you   green   patrolled by the same crazy cowboys?

Quién daría por esas auras manchadas?

Quién daría algo por esas auras manchadas que las
vacas mugiendo dejan libres en los blancos espacios no
regidos de la muerte de sus perseguidores?

I.   La fuga de esas vacas es en la muerte no regida del
     vaquero   Por eso no mugen y son simbólicas

II. Iluminadas   en la muerte de sus perseguidores
     Agrupando símbolos

III. Retornando de esos blancos espacios no regidos
     a través de los blancos espacios de la muerte de Ud.
     que está loco   al revés   delante de ellas

Daría Ud. algo por esas azules auras que las vacas
mugiendo dejan libres   cerradas   y donde Ud. está en
su propio más allá   muerto   imaginario   regresando de
esas persecuciones?

Who would give for those spotted auras?

Who would give something for those spotted auras that the
mooing cows let loose in the white spaces not
patrolled by the death of their persecutors?

I. The fugue of those cows is in the death not patrolled by
    the cowboy   That's why they don't moo and are symbolic

II. Enlightened   in the death of their persecutors
    Grouping symbols

III. Returning from those unpatrolled white spaces
     through those white spaces of the death of you
     who's crazy   inside out   before them

Would you give something for those blue auras that the cows
mooing let loose   enclosed   and where you are in
your own beyond   dead   imaginary   returning from
those persecutions?

EPÍLOGO

Hoy laceamos este animal imaginario
que correteaba por el color blanco

EPILOGUE

Today we tie up this imaginary animal
that ran freely through the color white

MI AMOR DE DIOS

MY LOVE OF GOD

PAMPAS

Áreas de Desvarío (I)

Áreas de Pasión (II)

Áreas de Muerte (III)

TODA UNA PAMPA TU ALMA CHUPADA DIME QUE NO TUS
ENROJECIDOS OJOS

PAMPAS

Areas of Delirium (I)

Areas of Passion (II)

Areas of Death (III)

ALL A PAMPA YOUR SUCKED-UP SOUL TELL ME IT'S NOT SO YOUR
SWOLLEN EYES

LOS CAMPOS DEL HAMBRE

Áreas N = El Hambre de Mi Corazón

Áreas N = Campos N El Hambre de

Áreas N =

y el Hambre Infinita de Mi Corazón

THE FIELDS OF HUNGER

Areas N = The Hunger of My Heart

Areas N = Fields N The Hunger of

Areas N =

and the Infinite Hunger of My Heart

LOS CAMPOS DEL DESVARÍO

N = 1
La locura de mi obra

N =
La locura de la locura de la locura de la

N

THE FIELDS OF DELIRIUM

N = 1
The madness of my work

N =
The madness of the madness of the madness of the

N

LAS LLANURAS DEL DOLOR

eli

eli

y dolor

THE PLAINS OF PAIN

eli

eli

and pain

MI AMOR DE DIOS

MY LOVE OF GOD

LA VIDA NUEVA

THE NEW LIFE

INFERNO

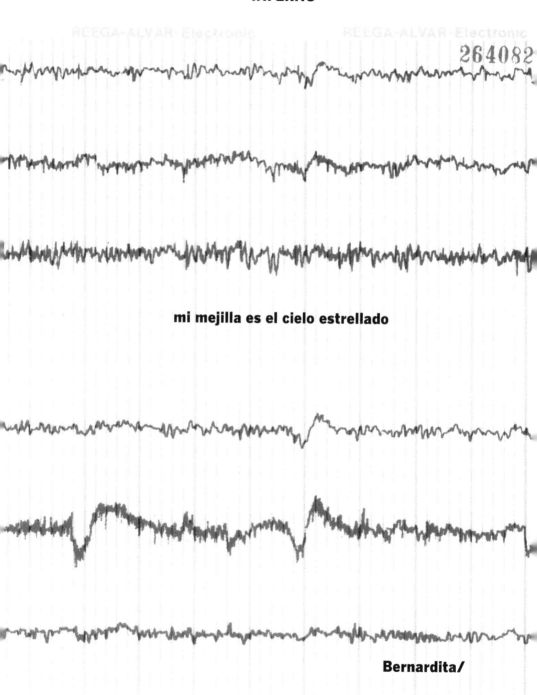

mi mejilla es el cielo estrellado

Bernardita/

INFERNO

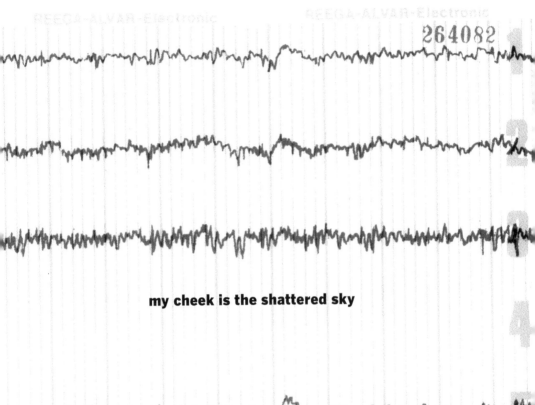

264082

my cheek is the shattered sky

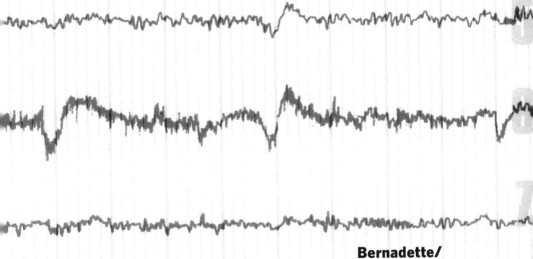

Bernadette/

PURGATORIO

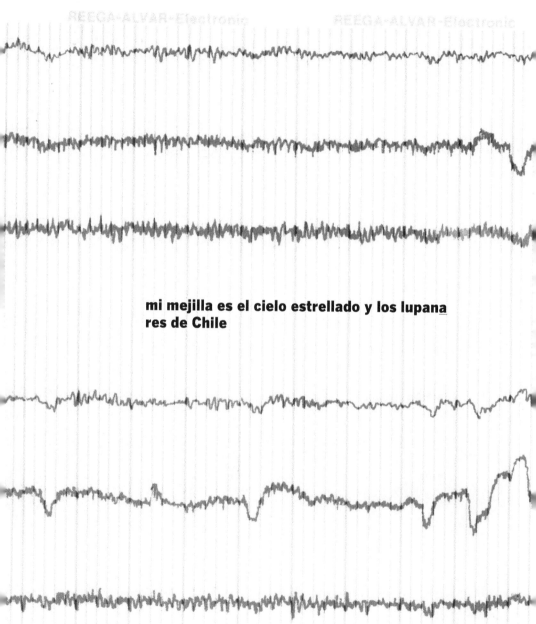

mi mejilla es el cielo estrellado y los lupana
res de Chile

Santa Juana/

PURGATORY

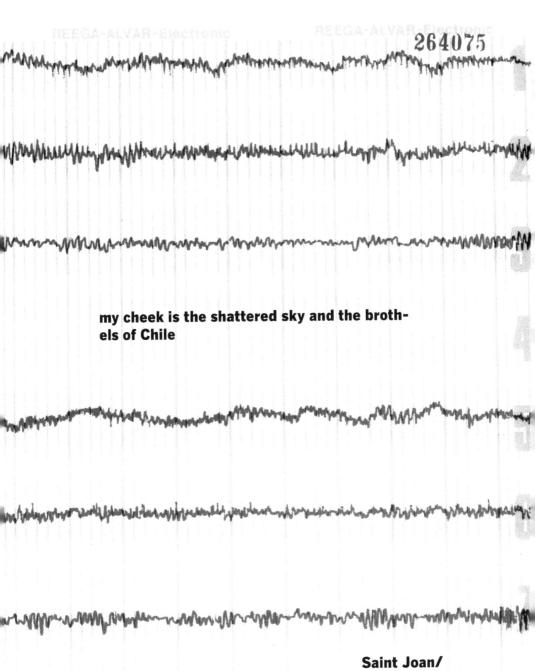

264075

my cheek is the shattered sky and the broth-
els of Chile

Saint Joan/

PARADISO

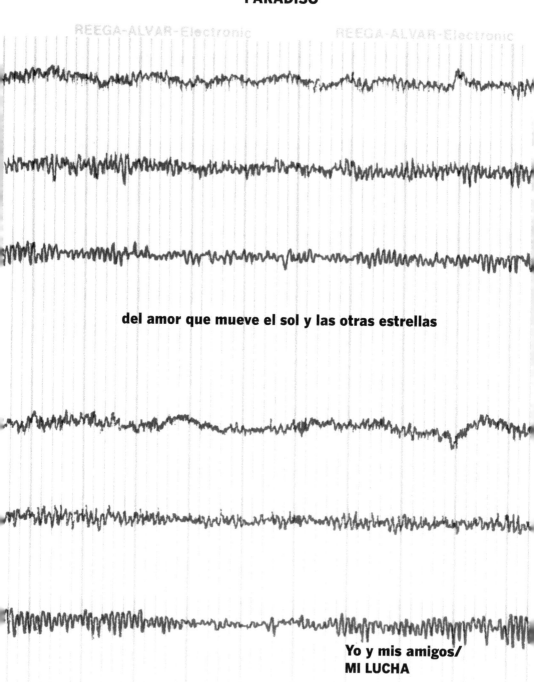

del amor que mueve el sol y las otras estrellas

Yo y mis amigos/
MI LUCHA

PARADISE

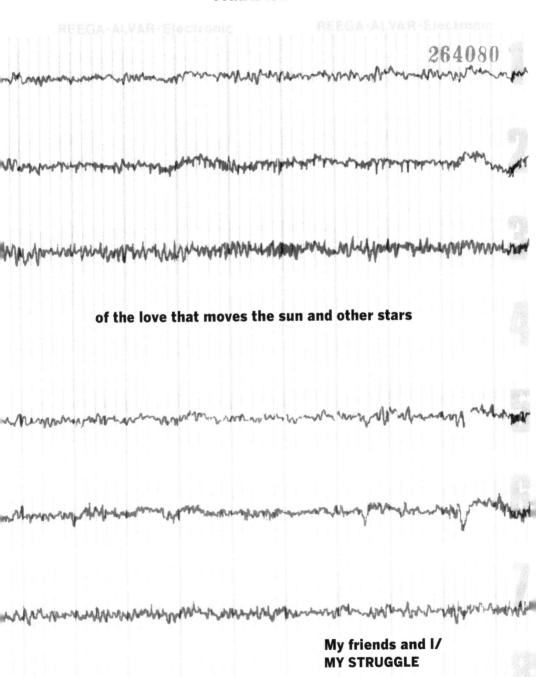

264080

of the love that moves the sun and other stars

**My friends and I/
MY STRUGGLE**

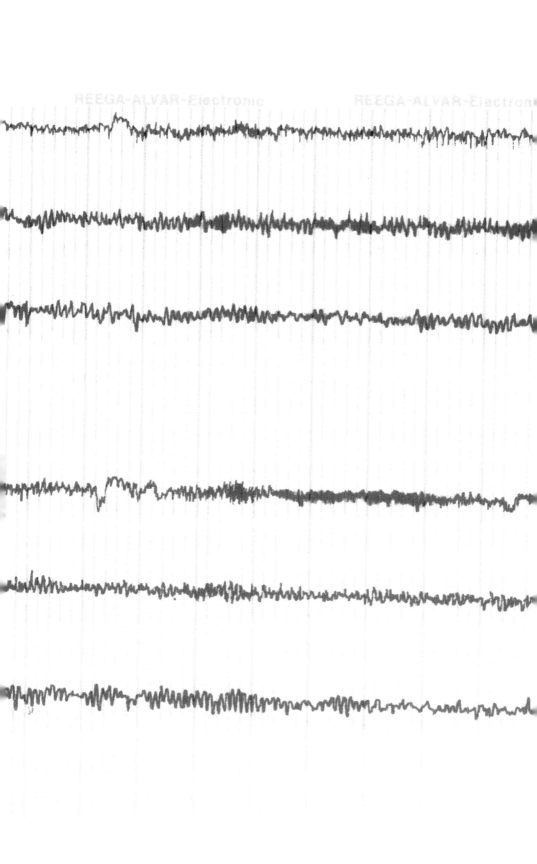

NOTES

DEVOCIÓN, p. 4

Diamela Eltit, a novelist and professor at the Universidad Tecnológica Metropolitana del Estado de Chile, was Zurita's romantic partner from 1975 to 1985. Zurita's first two volumes of poetry, *Purgatorio* (1979) and *Anteparaíso* (1982), are dedicated to her. Born in 1949 in Santiago, Chile, Eltit published many novels, including *Lumpérica* (1983), *Por la patria* (1986), *El cuarto mundo* (1988), *El padre mío* (1989), *Vaca sagrada* (1991), *El infarto del alma* (1994), *Los vigilantes* (1994), *Los trabajadores de la muerte* (1998), *Mano de obra* (2002), *Puño y letra* (2005), and *Jamás el fuego nunca* (2007). In 1979 Eltit and Zurita, along with visual artists Lotty Rosenfeld and Juan Castillo and sociologist Fernando Barcells, formed the Colectivo de Acciones de Arte (CADA).

EN EL MEDIO DEL CAMINO, p. 6

"EN EL MEDIO DEL CAMINO" is a direct reference to the first three lines of Dante Alighieri's *La Divina Commedia* (c. 1308–1321): "Nel mezzo del cammin di nostra vita / mi ritrovai per una selva oscura / ché la diritta via era smarrita." I have translated "EN EL MEDIO DEL CAMINO" as "IN THE MIDDLE OF THE ROAD" to emphasize, at this point in the text, a physical location. However, the emphasis on and sense of the word "camino" fluctuates throughout *Purgatory*. For example, on page 11, I have rendered "camino" as "way." In this context, "camino" suggests a spiritual and psychological journey.

III, p. 14

The use of the nominalized adjective "iluminada," as opposed to the noun "iluminación," feminizes the poetic voice, the "I," and thus confuses any assumption regarding the speaker's gender. But here Zurita is also referring to the Buddhist idea of enlightenment. I have thus rendered "esta iluminada" as "this enlightened woman."

LXIII, p. 20

When "mancha" refers directly to a cow, I have rendered the word as "spot." However, at other moments throughout the text, I have translated "mancha" as "stain."

COMO UN SUEÑO, p. 28

The Desert of Atacama, the most arid region on Earth, is located in northern Chile. Its vast pampas of salt basins, sand, and lava flows extend approximately six hundred miles (one thousand kilometers) from the center of Chile in Copiapó to Peru and, horizontally, from the Andes to the Pacific Ocean. Throughout the desert, towns such as Chacabuco and Pisagua were developed, from the late nineteenth century until the 1940s, as centers for the mining of nitrate ore. Chacabuco and Pisagua were used as concentration camps by Pinochet's dictatorial regime.

COMO UN SUEÑO, p. 30

Here "son" (they are), the third-person plural form of "ser," does not agree with the proper noun "Desierto de Atacama." "[S]on puras manchas" (they are pure stains) is rendered figuratively as "it's nothing but stains." A similar grammatical juxtaposition can be found on page 33, where I have rendered "YO USTED Y LA NUNCA SOY LA VERDE PAMPA EL/DESIERTO DE CHILE" as "I YOU AND NEVER I AM THE GREEN PAMPA THE/DESERT OF CHILE."

EL DESIERTO DE ATACAMA VII, p. 50

In the first lines of this poem, I have translated "mirar" as "look" to suggest the physical turning of the head, the opening of the eyes, and so on, derived from an internal *decision* to do so. The word *see* would have a more passive connotation. (I can see something without deciding to look at it.) In Chilean Spanish, "facha" is similar to the word *look*, as in the particular quality of a person's appearance. In Spanish, through assonance, the repetition of "facha" causes the word, concept, and image to become more porous as it sounds in relation to words such as "devenga" (becomes), "extendida" (extends), and "soledad" (solitude). Conversely, if we were to translate "facha" as "look," its repetition would become evocative of commercialism, the fashion industry, and the superficial in the same way that looks or images are continuously brought out for public consumption. I have translated "facha" as "form" because, like "facha," "form" opens up through assonance to "Crown," "thorn," "forever," and "cross." In this context, "form" also suggests the breakdown and the piecing back together of actual aesthetic, generic, physical, spiritual, and psychological forms.

VAMOS EL INCREÍBLE ACOSO DE LA VACA, p. 68

The Aramaic phrase "Eli Eli / lamma sabacthani" is attributed to Jesus and recorded in the New Testament: "At about three o'clock Jesus cried out with a loud shout, 'Eli, Eli, lamma sabacthani?' which means, 'My God, my God, why did you abandon me?'" (Matthew 27:46; Mark 15:34). In Spanish, "Eli" is often rendered as "Padre" (Father), as opposed to "Dios" (God).

INFERNO, p. 90

"Estrellado" means "starry sky" as well as "fractured" or "ruptured." Here Zurita is referring to the first passage of *Purgatory:* "My friends think / I'm a sick woman / because I burned my cheek." I have rendered "estrellado" as "shattered" because in sound and image it is suggestive of a starry sky. Unlike "fractured" or "ruptured," "shattered" flattens the cheek and the sky into multiple pieces that are dispersed and uncontainable.

TRANSLATOR'S AFTERWORD
SPEAKING FROM THE WRECKAGE

On September 11, 1973, General Augusto Pinochet deposed Chile's demo-
cratically elected president, Salvador Allende. Supported by the CIA and
U.S. military forces, Pinochet halted the progress of Allende's socialist
platform and transformed Chile into an export-based neoliberal econ-
omy. The multifront coup began shortly before dawn, when the Chilean
armada occupied the town of Valparaíso. Soon after, the national air force
bombarded La Moneda, the presidential palace in Santiago, as well as
the surrounding plazas.[1] During the coup and throughout the ensuing sev-
enteen-year dictatorship, tens of thousands of people on the streets, in
factories, homes, and universities, were rounded up, detained, tortured,
murdered, and disappeared. The regime efficiently transformed naval
vessels, mining towns, and soccer stadiums into concentration camps.[2]
Artistic, literary, and cultural communities of discourse were disbanded
and purged, political parties were abolished, assemblies were prohibited,
and curfews were imposed. As it privatized and sold Chile's resources to
an international market, the brutal military junta clinched its power by
refiguring the terms of citizenship, effacing individual identity, and impos-
ing a culture of violence, fear, silence, and censorship.

At that time an engineering student at the Universidad Técnica Federico
Santa María in Valparaíso, Raúl Zurita was arrested on the morning of the
coup and detained and tortured in the hold of a ship called *Maipo*. "None
of the poetic forms I knew, nothing," Zurita reflects in the preface to this
edition, served to convey "our suffering, but also . . . a strange perpetuity
and survival. . . . I had to learn to speak again from total wreckage, almost
from madness, so that I could still say something to someone." Two years
later, *Manuscritos*, a literary journal at the University of Chile's Departa-

mento de Estudios Humanísticos, published "Áreas Verdes," "Green Areas," and "Mi Amor de Dios," "My Love of God," along with a series of poems by the already renowned Nicanor Parra. As a result of the publication, Cristián Hunneus was fired from his position as department chair. The department itself was disbanded and the building taken over by the Dirección de la Inteligencia National (DINA), Pinochet's National Intelligence Directorate, which was responsible for the majority of the disappearances, tortures, and assassinations carried out during the dictatorship.[3]

Despite this severe censorship, that same year Ignacio Valente, an influential literary critic of the journal *Mercurio,* wrote "El poeta Zurita," a highly favorable review consecrating the previously unknown author as the new poetic voice of Chile. *Mercurio* was a state-sponsored publication that apparently overlooked Zurita's implicit condemnation of the regime, instead emphasizing *Purgatory*'s Dantean and Christian themes. Zurita completed what would be one of Latin America's most visionary works of poetry in 1976. Supported by Valente as well as by Enrique Lihn and Eduardo Anguita, both important Chilean poets associated with the University of Chile's press, *Purgatory* was finally published by the Editorial Universitaria in 1979.[4]

Purgatory inaugurates the search for a language capable of comprehending and overcoming the traumatic life conditions under military rule in Chile. This groundbreaking volume of poetry was conceived as the first text of a Dantean trilogy that includes *Anteparaíso* (1982) and *La vida nueva* (1994). Written and published at the height of the dictatorship, *Anteparaíso* is a lamentation of "los chilenos destinos," "Chile's destinies," embodied in the cordilleras and beaches.[5] But it is also a reflection on individual will, communal responsibility, and hope. In 1982 Zurita had the first poem of *Anteparaíso* written over Queens, New York. An "homage to minorities throughout the world" and, in particular, to "the Hispanic population in the United States," the white smoke of five planes spelled out verses that include:

MI DIOS ES CÁNCER
MI DIOS ES VACÍO

MI DIOS ES HERIDA
MI DIOS ES GHETTO . . .[6]

MY GOD IS CANCER
MY GOD IS EMPTINESS
MY GOD IS WOUND
MY GOD IS GHETTO . . .

Photographs of the event fill the white and sky blue pages of the book itself. Published after redemocratization, *La vida nueva*, "The New Life," is a relentless gallop of poetic voices, a meditation on shame and a requiem, a cathedral of testimonies, literature, and history that merge in a landscape of rivers, cordilleras, oceans, and sky. The last verse of this text, "Ni pena ni miedo," "No shame no fear," monumentally inscribed by Zurita in the Desert of Atacama in 1993, concludes this epic tour de force.

During the past thirty years, Zurita has published numerous volumes of poetry and prose, including *El paraíso está vacío* (1984), *Canto a su amor desaparecido* (1985), *Canto de los ríos que se aman* (1993), *Poemas militantes* (2000), *El día más blanco* (2000), *INRI* (2003), *Mi mejilla es el cielo estrellado* (2004), *Los poemas muertos* (2006), *Los países muertos* (2006), and *Poemas de amor* (2007).[7] In the late 1970s and early 1980s, along with visual artists Lotty Rosenfeld and Juan Castillo, writer Diamela Eltit, and sociologist Fernando Barcells, Zurita founded an art action group known as CADA, the Colectivo de acciones de arte. CADA staged protests, performances, art exhibits, and literary readings in streets, brothels, and the sky. Zurita's recitals throughout the world and his experimentation with poetic forms, sites of language and materials, have drawn thousands together to experience a poetry that can be held as much within the hand and mind as in the earth and atmosphere. And yet, despite this remarkable breadth of poetic endeavors, he believes, as he says in the preface, that all of it is "an extension of *Purgatory* zones," as if it were written to represent a memory and the wreckage that followed.

Purgatory is an unprecedented rendering of the memory that was as much Zurita's as it was Chile's. To "speak again," to "say something to someone," Zurita pieced together multiple forms and voices. The result is an uncanny postmodern collage of seemingly unrelated registers, languages, and documents that range from an ID card photo, a handwritten letter, and encephalograms to Dante and Neruda, non-Euclidean geometries, and the pathos of a cow. The desolate and unsettling poetic voice expands and contracts as it traverses identities and landscapes, figuring as masculine and feminine, saint and whore, human, animal, self and other. The poet emerges as everyone and everything everywhere.

This juxtaposition of voices is one of the most important literary achievements developed in *Purgatory* and later fully realized in his most recent works, *Zurita/In Memoriam* (2007) and *Las ciudades de agua* (2007). The technique is an approach to an acute crisis of meaning at a specific historical moment. But it is also Zurita's response to a fundamental quandary of poetry and philosophy reflected in writers such as Friedrich Nietzsche, Martin Heidegger, T.S. Eliot, Pablo Neruda, and Nicanor Parra. This is the question of an individual's inability to speak of a cohesive self and, more difficult still, of a cohesive *other*. How can a poet express memories and experiences if he cannot grasp his own? And if he does attempt to express those memories and experiences, what language can he use? Such challenges reveal the "I" of poetic voice, its unity, and the grammatical structures that sustain that unity, as profoundly unstable. What poetic forms, then, could manifest this instability, this breakdown, that Zurita understood as the "wreckage"?

PABLO NERUDA AND NICANOR PARRA

In Chile, Pablo Neruda (1904–1973), to whom Zurita is often compared, and Nicanor Parra (b. 1914) engage similar uncertainties regarding the consistency, efficacy, and ultimate purpose of the poetic voice. Neruda's "No hay olvido," literally "There Is No Forgetfulness," of *Residencia en la tierra 2 (1931–1935),* for example, demonstrates the "I" as incapable of finding a language to adequately address "where [it] has been":

Si me preguntáis en dónde he estado
debo decir "Sucede".
Debo de hablar del suelo que oscurecen las piedras,
del río que durando se destruye:
no sé sino las cosas que los pájaros pierden,
el mar dejado atrás, o mi hermana llorando.
Por qué tantas regiones, por qué un día
se junta con un día? Por qué una negra noche
se acumula en la boca? Por qué muertos?
Si me preguntáis de dónde vengo, tengo que conversar con cosas rotas,
con utensilios demasiado amargos,
con grandes bestias a menudo podridas
y con mi acongojado corazón.[8]

If you ask me where I've been
I should say "Things happen."
I should speak of the ground darkened by stones,
of the river that enduring destroys itself:
I know only of things that birds misplace,
or the ocean left behind, or my sister crying.
Why so many regions, why does a day
meet another day? Why does a black night
accumulate in my mouth? Why the dead?
If you ask me where I come from, I have to converse with broken things,
with utensils that are too bitter,
with great beasts often rotten
and with my inconsolable heart.[9]

Neruda's memory of the self—"where I've been" and "where I come from"—
is answered as a series of "things"—"broken," misplaced, left behind—that
"happen." These "broken things" with which the poet "must converse" are
a registry of inadequate formal resources, such as "utensils" and "beasts"
that are "too bitter" and "rotten" to provide mnemonic assistance or physi-
cal sustenance. For Neruda, this is the memory of Latin America and the

search for origins that might constitute a cohesive individual or collective mnemonic narrative. But the poetic excavation of such a narrative reveals only residual fragments of the past that accumulate over time. Inherent in this incoherent memory of the self is that of the other—"my sister's crying"—who is either incapable of expressing her own sorrow through language or is simply incapable of being heard. Indeed, Neruda later shifts his focus from the question of how to converse with broken things and a broken past to what he recognizes as the more urgent issue of how to speak of and for others. In *Odas elementales* (1954), the poet of *Canto General* (1950) declares himself an "Invisible Man" who will "sing with all men":

> dadme
> las luchas
> de cada día
> porque ellas son mi canto,
> y así andaremos juntos,
> codo a codo,
> todos los hombres,
> mi canto los reúne:
> el canto del hombre invisible
> que canta con todos los hombres.[10]

> give me
> the struggles
> of each day
> because they are my song,
> and in this way we'll go together,
> arm in arm,
> all men,
> my song unites them:
> the song of the invisible man
> that sings with all men.

However hopeful, Neruda's "invisible man" is anything but hidden. After all, the poet's imperative and the poem's form have the unlimited capacity to "unite" all "struggles." That is, even though the poetic voice describes what it will do, it does not formally enact the proposition.

While Neruda's "I" attempts to subsume the voices and struggles of all men, Nicanor Parra adopts a conversational language to ridicule the idea of a poet's inherent ability and even right to articulate his own experience, much less someone else's. Published the same year as *Odas elementales*, "Rompecabezas"—"Puzzle" or, literally, "Headbreakers"—of *Poemas y antipoemas* understands words as inadequate, hackneyed material crudely taken to represent other materials:

> No doy a nadie el derecho.
> Adoro un trozo de trapo.
> Traslado tumbas de lugar. . . .
>
> Yo digo una cosa por otra.[11]

> I don't yield to anyone.
> I adore a piece of rag.
> I move tombs from here to there. . . .
>
> I say one thing for another.

Like Neruda, whose poetic voice converses with broken things, the poet here is a hoarder of "tombs" and "rags" who is incapable of piecing together the past to figure a cohesive present. Parra's "I" is a collection of failed metonymies and discursive debris because it will always signal something irretrievable, impossible to fully re-member and therefore to convey. Like tombs of civilizations past, moved from here to there, that no longer hold the dead, words no longer hold memories because they have lost their original usefulness. In "El soliloquio del individuo," "The Individual's Soliloquy," Parra flatly relates "I" the "Individual" to the ineffectual search for memory:

> Yo soy el Individuo.
> Bien.
> Mejor es tal vez que vuelva a ese valle,

A esa roca que me sirvió de hogar,
Y empiece a grabar de nuevo,
De atrás para adelante grabar
El mundo al revés.
Pero no: la vida no tiene sentido.[12]

I am the Individual.
OK.
I better get back to that valley,
To that rock that was my home,
And begin to record again,
Back and forth record
The world upside down.
But no: life has no meaning.

Here the "Individual" attempts to "record" memory, to constitute a trajec-
tory of meaning, but that effort proves impossible. The goal to locate a his-
torical or mnemonic narrative—Neruda's "where I've been" and "where I
come from"—that manages to convey "I" the "Individual" is futile because
"life" itself "has no meaning." That is, memory and history cannot find a
narrative or poetic form because "life" cannot be sequenced, ordered, or
made logical in any way.

PURGATORY

Zurita sought Neruda's communion of voices in texts such as *Odas ele-
mentales* but ultimately concluded that the poet can only speak of the
other's pain if his own voice is broken. Often adopting Parra's restrained
conversational language, he builds poems from discursive and formal
"tombs" and "rags" in order to assemble memory *without* needing to con-
vey a cohesive narrative of the self. Unlike Neruda and Parra, Zurita never
struggles with the loss of self-knowledge implicit in the "wreckage." That
is, the disintegration of the "I" of poetic voice becomes the poet's oppor-
tunity for intersubjectivity, and, more important, for empathy rather than
anxiety. Because "none of the poetic forms [he] knew, nothing" could ade-

quately convey the wreckage, Zurita's aim was to generate a combination of poetic forms and voices that seek Neruda's unity *through* the wreckage. Consider poem "III" of *Purgatory*:

> Todo maquillado contra los vidrios
> me llamé esta iluminada dime que no
> el Súper Estrella de Chile
> me toqué en la penumbra   besé mis piernas
>
> Me he aborrecido tanto estos años[13]

> All made-up face against the glass
> I called myself this enlightened woman tell me it's not so
> the Super Star of Chile
> I touched myself in the shadows   I kissed my legs
>
> I've hated myself so much these years

Zurita uses the feminine, "esta iluminada," "this enlightened woman," along with the extremes of masquerade, denigration, and self-love to break down the "I's" centripetal force. "Destrozado," or "smashed," in poem "XXII," the "I" here speaks to, aggrandizes, and detests itself through a colloquialism that is, simultaneously, enlightened. In poem "LXIII" the poetic voice conveys the pathetic and humble dream of a cow:

> Hoy soñé que era Rey
> me ponían una piel a manchas blancas y negras
> Hoy mujo con mi cabeza a punto de caer
> mientras las campanadas fúnebres de la iglesia
> dicen que va a la venta la leche[14]

> Today I dreamed that I was King
> they were dressing me in black-and-white spotted pelts
> Today I moo with my head about to fall
> as the church bells' mournful clanging
> says that milk goes to market

Here Zurita converges the sacrificial figure of a "King" whose head "falls" like Christ and a cow lamenting the sale of her milk. The "I" coalesces identities, impossible dreams, and oppression, while the church bells clearly mark the religion of institutional time and the buying and selling of goods.

Zurita sets institutional time against individual memory by delineating the latter as the infinite possibility of experiences that constitute the self, *regardless* of institutional time. Perhaps we can understand this concept more clearly through the final verse of "Desiertos," "Deserts," composed of a series of three poems, each called "Cómo un sueño," "Like a Dream," in which Zurita fuses multiple pronouns and time with the landscape: "YO USTED Y LA NUNCA SOY LA VERDE PAMPA EL/DESIERTO DE CHILE."[15] ("I YOU AND NEVER I AM THE GREEN PAMPA THE/DESERT OF CHILE"). If "I" and "you" hold individual memory, "never" is the prospect of individual and collective memory held within the landscape. For "never" is the dissolution of institutional time—"church-bell" time—that ushers forth absolute historical memory.

Paul Ricoeur's considerations in "Personal Memory, Collective Memory" are helpful here as we address the issue of pronoun usage and the quandary of mnemonic articulation. Ricoeur asks, "Why should memory be attributed only to me, to you, to her or to him, in the singular of the three grammatical persons capable of referring to themselves, of addressing another as you (in the singular), or of recounting the deeds of the third party in a narrative in the third person singular? And why could the attribution not be made directly to us, to you in the plural, to them?"[16] This is the poet's grammatical problem that is also, Ricoeur suggests, inextricably linked to the most basic philosophical questions regarding subjectivity, consciousness, the identity of the self, as John Locke called it, and again, an individual's ability to convey his or her own memory vis-à-vis a collective memory, church-bell time, or the distinct memories of others. "I YOU AND NEVER I AM" fastens memory and grammatical structures to the use of pronouns and, ultimately, the landscape, "THE GREEN PAMPA THE/DESERT OF CHILE."

I will comment on this convergence of voice and landscape below.

For now, let us note that while the progression of verses throughout this avant-garde text is not completely grammatical, in general, grammar and syntax sustain the poems' intelligibility. This is because *Purgatory* is not a text of failed forms. It is a vision of manifold forms—a photograph, a letter, non-Euclidean geometry—that need and seek one another to create a cohesive whole that, for Zurita, is the ideal union of art and life itself. The move toward the communion of forms and voices is a response to the segregation of people imposed by dictatorial violence as well as Zurita's condemnation of capitalism and the division of people into classes. But we can also understand this communion as a resistance to more general, and nonetheless destructive, privileging of discursive and analytical methods, particularly science and technology. Thus, an encephalogram, a machine used to trace the structure and electrical activity of the mind, is contrasted at the end of *Purgatory* with Zurita's cheek and the sky—"mi mejilla es el cielo estrellado," "my cheek is the shattered sky."[17] Developed at the end of the nineteenth century, the encephalogram is a tool used by the contemporary field of cognitive science, the study of the nature of intelligence. We can trace cognitive science to the philosophical investigations of the nature of human knowledge, to Plato and Aristotle, René Descartes, John Locke, Immanuel Kant, and more recently Martin Heidegger and Hannah Arendt. Cognitive science was coined as a term and established as a field in 1973. Thus, the images of the encephalogram, an instrument used to trace what is most hidden and silent within the complex processes of our minds, is juxtaposed against an external mark of effacement (shattered cheek) and the landscape (shattered sky). Language, technology, an individual human face: What form can express the landscape of the mind, the distinct electrical activity of our suffering, of our thoughts, of who we are and of how we speak of where we have been?

It is indeed the landscape that Zurita offers as the ultimate communal space in which individual and multiple voices, forms, and memories coalesce. In "El Desierto de Atacama VII," the poetic voice invites us to look on, to collectively witness the desert and the sky, imbued as much with the wreckage of segregation—"our loneliness"—as with the impossible dream beyond suffering, beyond formal segregation.

i. Miremos entonces el Desierto de Atacama

ii. Miremos nuestra soledad en el desierto

Para que desolado frente a estas fachas el paisaje
devenga una cruz extendida sobre Chile y la soledad de mi
facha vea entonces el redimirse de las otras fachas: mi
propia Redención en el Desierto

iii. Quién diría entonces del redimirse de mi facha

iv. Quién hablaría de la soledad del desierto

Para que mi facha comience a tocar tu facha y tu facha
a esa otra facha y así hasta que todo Chile no sea sino
una sola facha con los brazos abiertos: una larga facha
coronada de espinas[18]

i. Let's look then at the Desert of Atacama

ii. Let's look at our loneliness in the desert

So that desolate before these forms the landscape becomes
a cross extended over Chile and the loneliness of my form
then sees the redemption of the other forms: my own
Redemption in the Desert

iii. Then who would speak of the redemption of my form

iv. Who would tell of the desert's loneliness

So that my form begins to touch your form and your form
that other form like that until all of Chile is nothing but
one form with open arms: a long form crowned with thorns

In a direct allusion to the crucifixion of Christ "crowned with thorns," Zurita
unbinds Christ from the sacrifice Christianity demands of him. Why should
one good son die for so many? "So that my form begins to touch your form
and your form / that other form" imagines a shared experience and recog-

nition of individual pain. Only such a boundless space could hold this ideal merging and redemption. This is not, however, a religious redemption. It is a hope and faith in the ultimate ability of expressive forms, despite their limits. As Francine Masiello observes, "Zurita persuades us that . . . new combinations of language and form will always emerge to speak of pain, loss, and denigration."[19]

What begins in *Purgatory* as a series of juxtapositions becomes, in *Zurita/In Memoriam* and *Las ciudades de agua,* a complete fusion of multiple voices that speak, not as a collage, but as one. In these texts the poetic voice moves us fluidly between the living and the dead, mountain summit and city street, masculine and feminine, and even national affiliations. In the following passages, Akira Kurosawa, the renowned Japanese film director, shares the same "I" as "Zurita" and the typewriter salesman who speaks frozen beneath the snow. Consider "Sueño 354/a Kurosawa," "Dream 354/to Kurosawa":

> Yo sobreviví
> a una dictadura, pero no a la vergüenza. Años después,
> cuando me llegó a mí el turno, su cara se me vino encima
> como una montaña blanca de sal. Quise escribirlo, pero
> las palabras, como vísceras humeantes, llegaron
> muertas a mis dedos. Mi nombre: Akira Kurosawa.[20]

> I survived a dictatorship, but not
> the shame. Many years later, when it was
> my turn, her face came down upon me like
> a white mountain of salt. I wanted to write it, but
> the words, like smoldering entrails, arrived
> dead to my fingers. My name: Akira Kurosawa.

And from "Sueño 35/a Kurosawa":

> La represión ha sido feroz y han arrojado los cuerpos
> sobre el mar y las montañas. Al levantarme observé

que no podía mover mis brazos encostrados bajo
la nieve. Kurosawa, le dije, yo era un simple vendedor
de máquinas de escribir y ahora estoy muerto y nieva.[21]

The repression has been ferocious and they've
thrown the bodies over the sea and the
mountains. As I get up I notice I cannot
move my arms frozen beneath the snow.
Kurosawa, I said, I was just a typewriter
salesman and now I'm dead and it snows.

Affiliations that determine how we delineate difference and division
through nation, body, gender, geography, trade, and genre, through the
living and the dead, are completely dissolved. The need to speak of pain
through the communion of form and voices is the groundwork for the dis-
solution first established in *Purgatory*.

In 2007 Ediciones Universidad Diego Portales released a new edition
of *Purgatory*. Read now, nineteen years after redemocratization, the new
edition reiterates the initial horror and protest of the forces that instigated
the coup. Even throughout Chile's transition to democracy, its government
and the US government are hesitant to acknowledge the extent of the
regime's brutality and the United States' direct monetary, military, and
ideological involvement. *Purgatory* reminds us. To access, display, and
recombine forms of representation, to break down and unbind elements
such as grammar, syntax, agreement of number and gender, is to under-
stand poetic voice as a mnemonic fabric. As we unbind and stitch back
together these elements, we alter the terms of history, the terms by which
we remember ourselves—our own voices and complex memories—in rela-
tion to one another.

THE TRANSLATABILITY OF *PURGATORY*

In "The Task of the Translator" Walter Benjamin suggests that "translation
is a mode," a manner in which something occurs or is experienced. What

occurs or what is experienced is "translatability," explains Benjamin, the manifestation of "a specific significance inherent in the original."[22] Thus, translatability is not the propensity for a text in its original language to be translated but what is revealed of a text and language *through* translation. The "specific significance" of a text, what is "manifest," is the "unforgettable," the "central reciprocal relationship between languages" because, writes Benjamin, "languages are not strangers to one another, but are, a priori and apart from all historical relationships, interrelated in what they want to express." Translation reveals an inherent, linguistic muscle memory of what Benjamin calls "intention." This intention is as unforgettable as it is beyond a univocal mnemonic or historical narrative.

Let me provide an example of what becomes unforgettable through the translatability of *Purgatory*. While translating a section from "Áreas verdes," I was faced with the specific problem of *vaca* and *vacío*:

> No hay domingos para la vaca:
> mugiendo despierta en un espacio vacío
> babeante   gorda   sobre esos pastos imaginarios[23]

How can we replicate the assonance and meaning of words that would directly translate into English as "cow" and "empty"? One possibility was "heifer" and "cipher," "heifer" meaning "a young female cow" and "cipher" meaning "zero," or "a person of no importance who has no will of her own." This would have been an appropriate solution if the poem only represented *vacas* who had not borne calves. Therefore, *vaca* demanded "cow." As I began to consider the etymology of "cow" to test my decision, an inevitable translatability emerged. We can trace *vaca* to the Latin *vacca* and *vacare*, "to vacate," to the Old English, Germanic, and Indo-European root shared by both the Latin *bos* and the Greek *bous*. "Cow" can also be traced to the Old Norse word *kúga*, which means "to oppress." And what word to use for *vacío*? Assonance led me to "hollow" because it rhymes with "cow." "Hollow" comes to us from the Old English word *holh*, which means "cave," and is related to the Latin *cavus*, like "cavern." It is associated in turn to the expression "cave in" or *calve*, which leads to the word "excavate," but also to the word "calf." So we have: *vaca-bos-bous-kúga*-cow-hollow-*holh*-cave-calf-oppressed:

> There are no Sundays for the cow:
> mooing awake in a hollow space
> drooling   heavy   throughout those imaginary pastures

This is translatability or translation as a mode, as a way in which what is unforgettable has occurred or is experienced. Both translation and poetry are modes, since they emphasize tracing, choosing, and reconfiguring connections and affiliations in order to access the unforgettable. This is their undeniable *intention.* That is, the intention of memory without history, Parra's tombs and rags that evoke the unforgettable at the same time that they manifest a crisis regarding how to speak the unforgettable as constitutive of the self. This is the translatability of *Purgatory,* of the wreckage that occurs, of where Zurita has been but what he cannot and yet, nonetheless, attempts to speak.

NOTES

1. For testimonies describing the first months of the coup, see Santiago Dowling, ed., *Chile, primavera negra: cara y cruz del golpe militar* (Buenos Aires: Rodolfo Alonso Editor, 1974).
2. Mary Louise Pratt associates the appropriation of public spaces of "political" and "nonpolitical citizenship" with the delineation of a "masculine nationality." She also observes that the regime's discursive authoritarian strategies were intended to establish women as the embodiments of a new nation. See "Overwriting Pinochet: Undoing the Culture of Fear in Chile," in *The Places of History: Regionalism Revisited in Latin America,* ed. Doris Sommer (Durham: Duke University Press, 1999), 25–27.
3. Raúl Zurita, e-mail to Anna Deeny, September 4, 2008.
4. Zurita, e-mail to Deeny, September 7, 2008.
5. Zurita, "Yo no quiero que mi amor se muera," in *Anteparaíso* (Madrid: Visor, 1991), 31. *Anteparaíso* was translated into English by Jack Schmidt in 1986. See *Anteparadise: A Bilingual Edition* (Berkeley and Los Angeles: University of California Press, 1986).
6. Zurita, "La vida nueva," in *Anteparaíso,* 24.
7. In 2009 Marick Press will publish William Rowe's translation of *INRI,* and

Action Books will publish Daniel Borzutzky's translation of *Canto a su amor desaparecido*.

8. Pablo Neruda, "No hay olvido," in *Residencia en la tierra 2 (1931–1935)* (Madrid: Ediciones Cátedra, 1958), 301–2.
9. Unless otherwise noted, this and all other poetry translations are my own.
10. Neruda, "El hombre invisible," in *Odas elementales* (Madrid: Ediciones Cátedra, 2005), 65.
11. Nicanor Parra, "Rompecabezas," in *Poemas y antipoemas* (Madrid: Ediciones Cátedra, 1988), 83.
12. Parra, "Soliloquio del individuo," in *Poemas y antipoemas,* 116.
13. Zurita, "III," in *Purgatorio* (Santiago: Ediciones Universidad Diego Portales, 2007), 16.
14. Zurita, "LXIII," in *Purgatorio,* 19.
15. Zurita, "Cómo un sueño," in *Purgatorio,* 27.
16. Paul Ricoeur, "Personal Memory, Collective Memory," in *Memory, History, Forgetting,* trans. Kathleen Blamey and David Pellauer (Chicago: University of Chicago Press, 2004), 93–94.
17. Zurita, "Inferno," in *Purgatorio,* 65.
18. Zurita, "El Desierto de Atacama VII," in *Purgatorio,* 38.
19. Francine Masiello, letter to University of California Press, March 30, 2008.
20. Zurita, "Sueño 354/a Kurosawa," in *Las ciudades de agua* (México D. F.: Ediciones Era, 2007), 21.
21. Zurita, "Sueño 35/a Kurosawa," in *Zurita/In Memoria* (Santiago: Ediciones Tácitas, 2007), 35.
22. Walter Benjamin, "The Task of the Translator," in *Illuminations,* ed. Hannah Arendt and trans. Harry Zohn (New York: Schocken Books, 2007), 71.
23. Zurita, "Han visto extenderse estos pastos infinitos?" in *Purgatorio,* 48.

DESIGNER: CLAUDIA SMELSER
TEXT: BENTON GOTHIC   DISPLAY: BANK GOTHIC
COMPOSITOR: BOOKMATTERS, BERKELEY
PRINTER AND BINDER: THOMSON-SHORE, INC.

Lightning Source UK Ltd.
Milton Keynes UK
UKHW010639161021
392317UK00001B/116